The N

Bayfield School

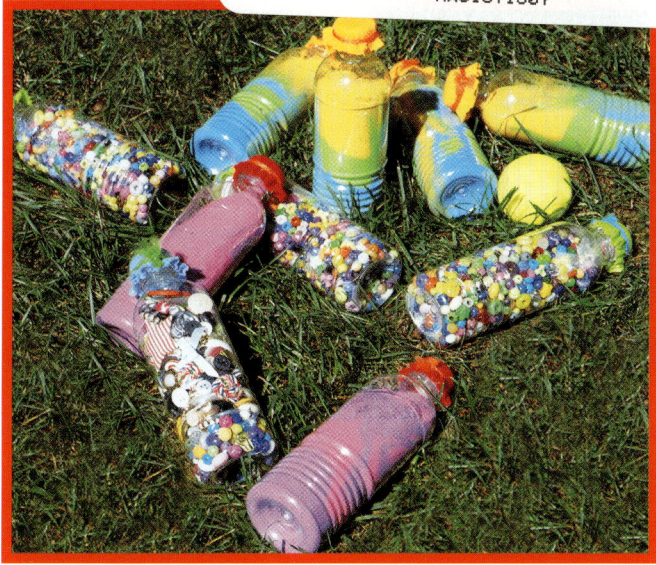

Barbara Taragan

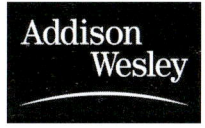

Toronto

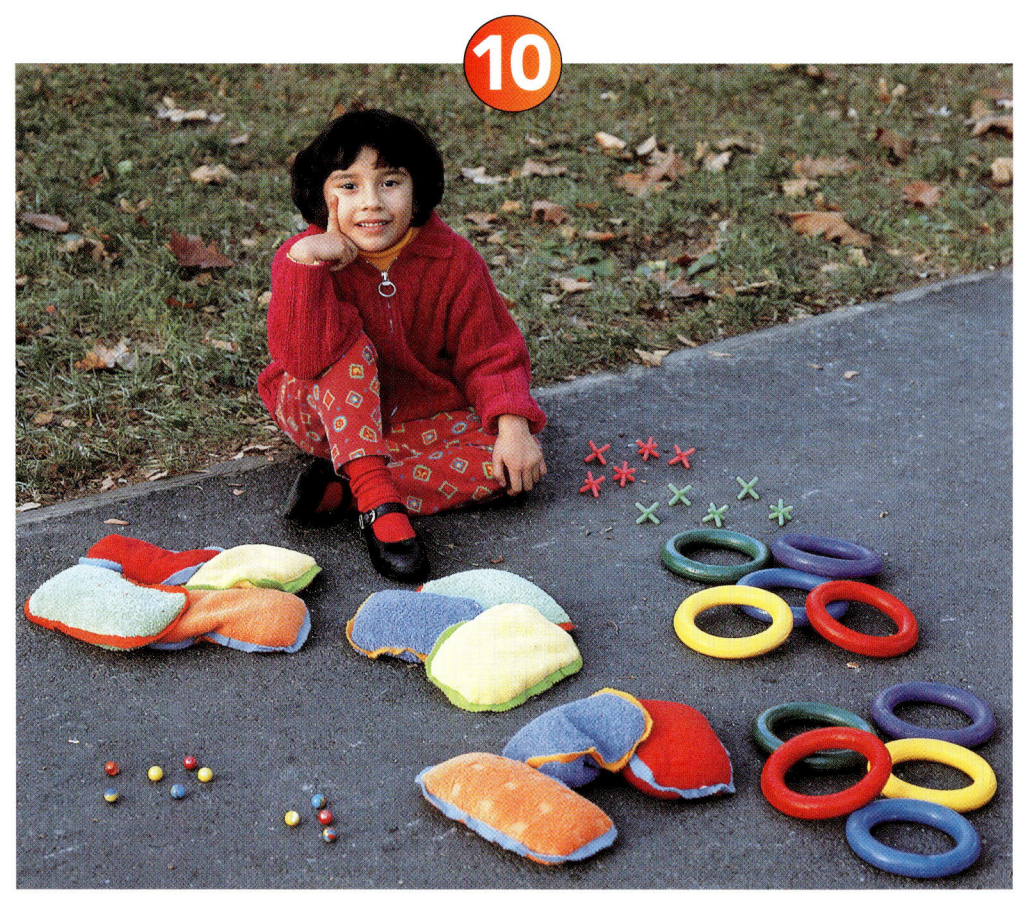

Can you make up games with ten?

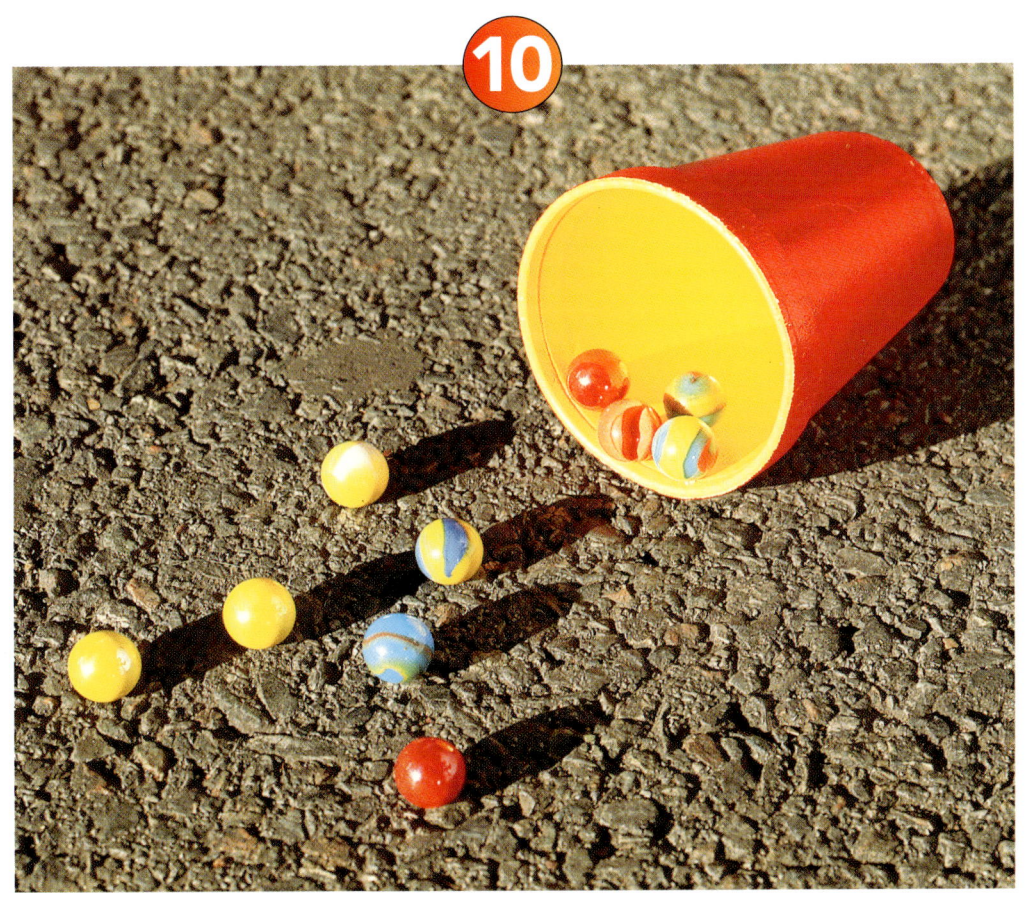

Can you roll ten marbles into a cup?

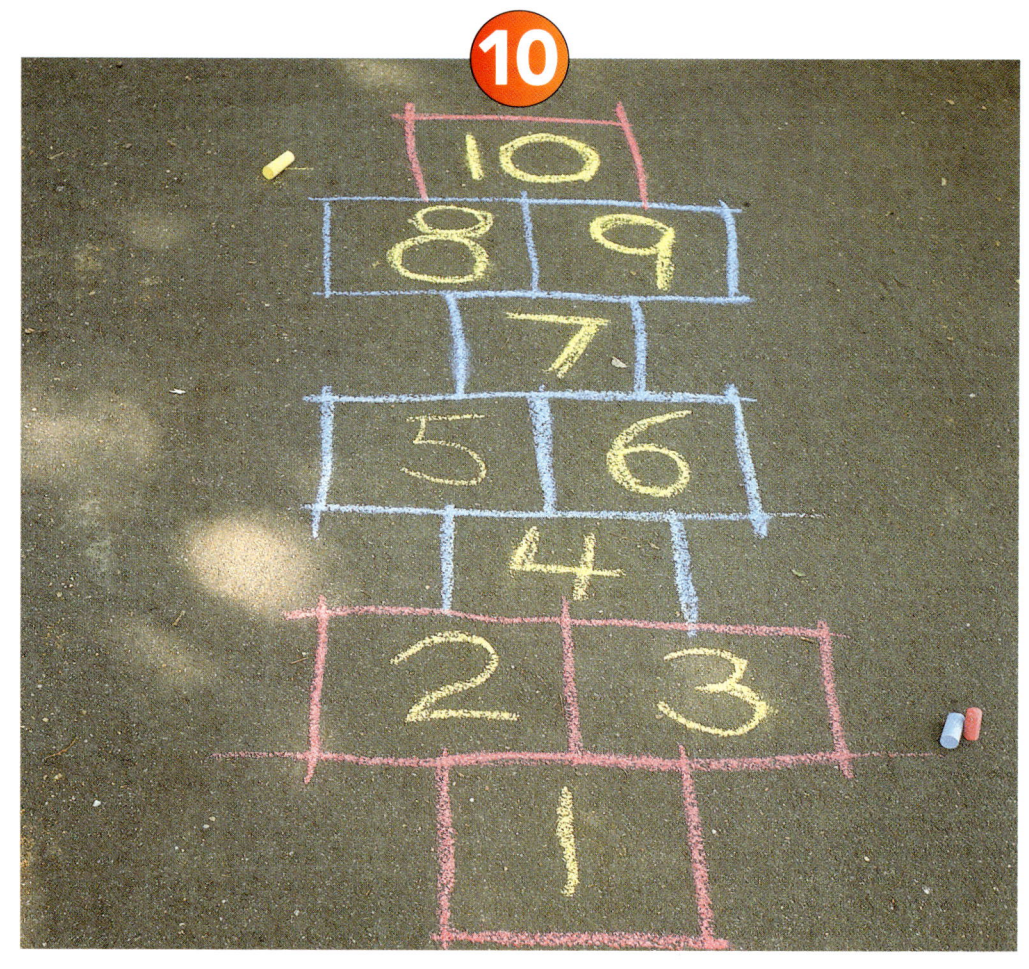

Can you hop in ten squares?

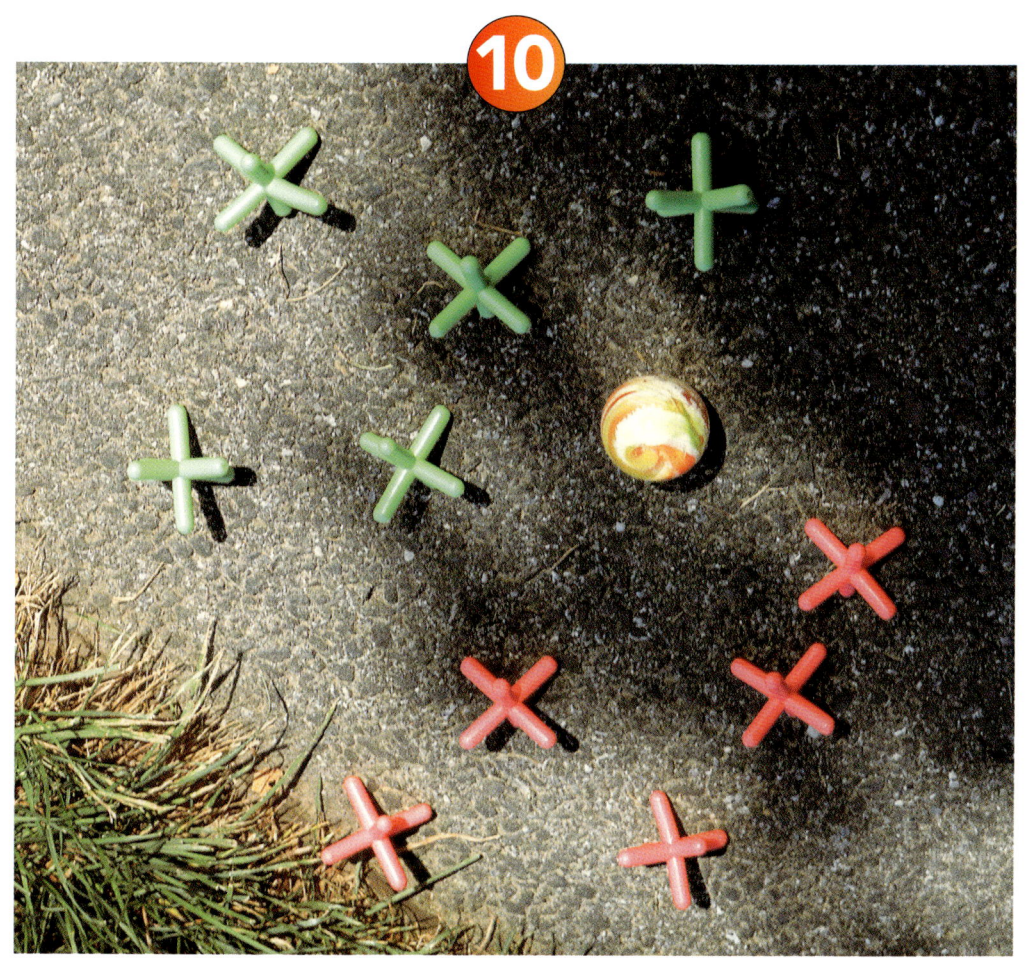

Can you pick up ten jacks?

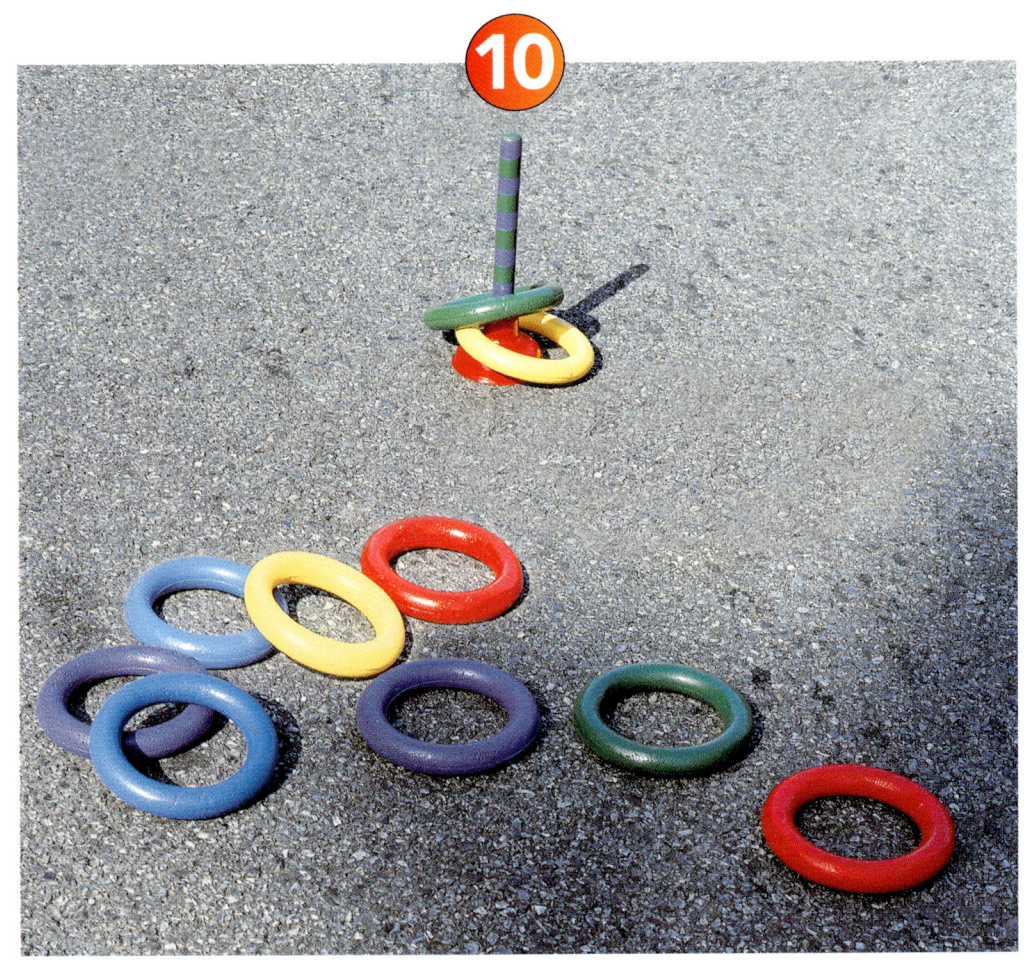

Can you toss ten rings?

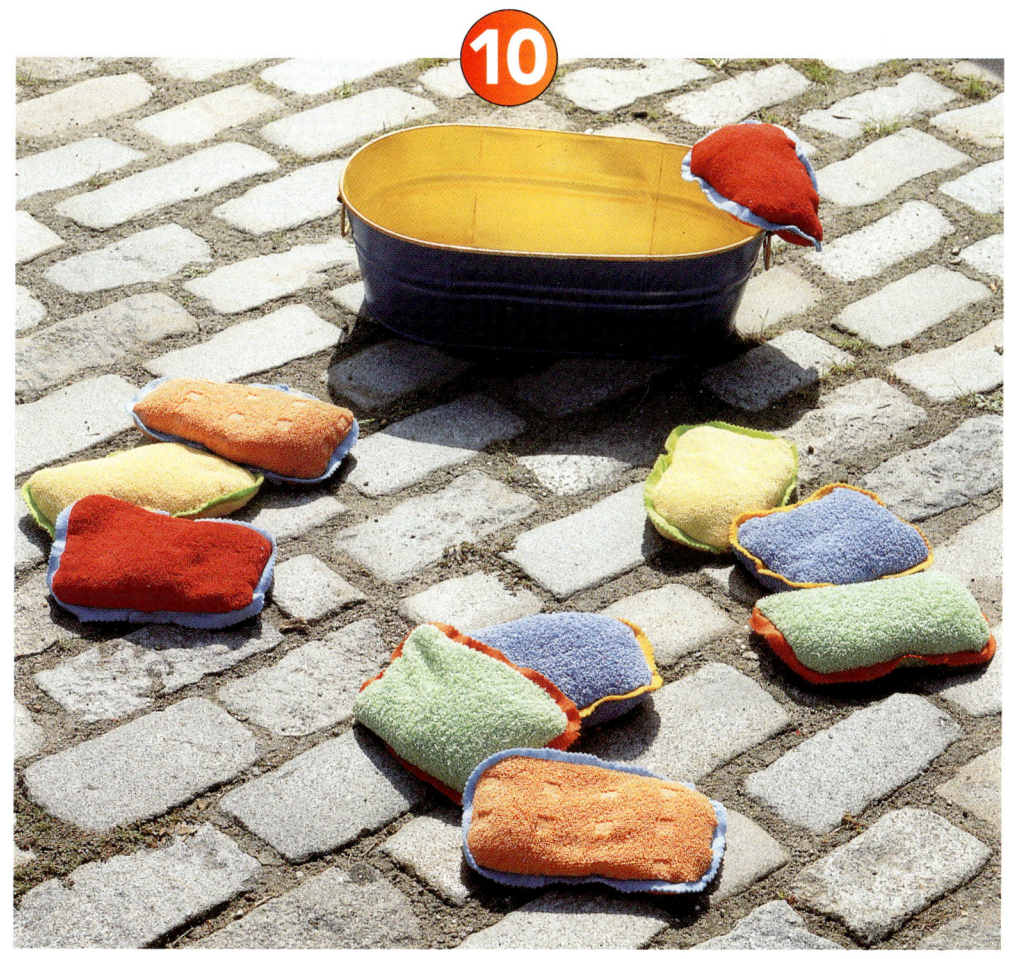

Can you toss ten beanbags?

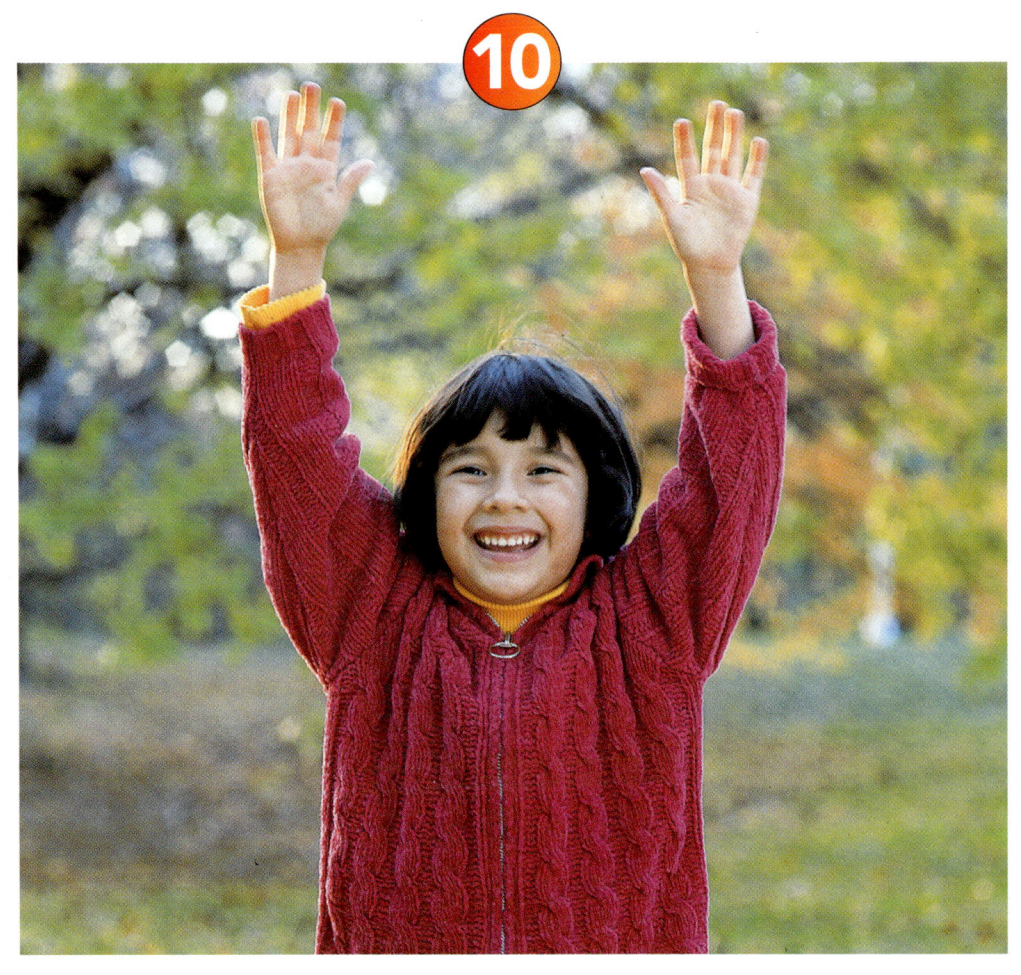

Then you can say, "I win!"